THESE MANY ROOMS

Also by Laure-Anne Bosselaar

Poetry

The Hour Between Dog & Wolf
Small Gods of Grief
A New Hunger

Anthologies

Night Out: Poems about Hotels, Motels, Restaurants & Bars,
      Edited with Kurt Brown
Outsiders: Poems about Rebels, Exiles and Renegades
Urban Nature: Poems about Wildlife in the City
Never Before: Poems about First Experiences

Translation

The Plural of Happiness: Selected Poems by Herman de Coninck,
      Translated from the Dutch with Kurt Brown

THESE MANY ROOMS

Laure-Anne Bosselaar

Four Way Books
Tribeca

Library of Congress Cataloging-in-Publication Data
Names: Bosselaar, Laure-Anne, 1943- author.
Title: These many rooms / Laure-Anne Bosselaar.
Description: New York, NY : Four Way Books, 2019.
Identifiers: LCCN 2018028710 | ISBN 9781945588273 (pbk. : alk. paper)
Classification: LCC PS3552.O772 A6 2019 | DDC 811/.54-dc23
LC record available at https://lccn.loc.gov/2018028710

Four Way Books is a not-for-profit literary press. We are grateful for the assistance
we receive from individual donors, public arts agencies, and private foundations.

This publication is made possible with public funds from the
National Endowment for the Arts

and from the New York State Council on the Arts, a state agency.

We are a proud member of the Community of Literary Magazines and Presses.

CONTENTS

III

Kurt Brown — ma lumière

(1944-2013)

et pour mon grand soleil

Tibo

I

ATTIC ROOM IN BELGIUM

Dust covers the window, but light slips through —
it always does — through cracks & under doors.

Every day at dusk, the sun, through branches,
hits a river's bend & sends silver slivers to the walls.

No one's there to see this. No one.
But it dances there anyway, that light,

& when the wind weaves waves into the water
it's as if lit syllables quivered on the bricks.

Then the sun sinks, swallowed by the dark. In that dark
more dust, more dust settles — sighs over everything.

There is no silence there: something always stirs
not far away. Small rags of noise.

Rilke said most people will know only a small corner of their room.

I read this long ago & still don't know

how to understand that word *only*.

I think of you, love — search for you in each room

that breathes between me & dusk, me & dust.

Love, torn corner from this life.

ON MY WALK TO THE HOSPITAL, DEATH

There it was,

        mired in the Styrofoam & syringes

    that the homeless left under an old,

hunchbacked oak.

Death in the fog, all silver

       & grisaille as it wreathes

& muffles children in the park.

I saw it

    in the needle, deep in the back

     of his hand. My love's.

     Fentanyl dripping

        no

        pain

        no

pain

no

in his vein.

Death in the still-life

the ward's window reflected:

an old woman bent over

her husband, her hand on his heart.

It faced us, there —

at the foot of the bed —

patient, nonchalant,

whistling softly through its teeth.

II

ROOMS REMEMBERED

[I needed, for months]

I needed, for months after he died, to remember our rooms —

  some lit by the trivial, others gentle with an obscurity

that comforted us: it hid our own darkness.

  So for months, duteous, I remembered:

rooms where friends lingered, rooms with our beds,

  with our books, rooms with curtains I sewed

from bright cottons. Tables of laughter,

  a chipped bowl in early light, black

branches by a window, bowing toward night, & those rooms,

  too, in which we came together

to be away from all — & sometimes from ourselves —

  I remembered that, also.

But tonight — as I lean into the doorway to his room

    & stare at dusk settled there —

what I remember best is how, to throw my arms around his neck,

    I needed to stand on the tips of my toes.

[This longing for him]

This longing for him, the choke in my throat again —

           enough, enough.

I throw a coat over my shoulders,

           close the door behind me, softly,

as if afraid to wake another ache.

           Another dawn. It'll seep into the sky

behind the palms. Fists in my pockets, I head east

           into this street

of bungalows as if I belonged here, among the hundred

           windows lit one by one, among the first

joggers & their dogs, past garages yawning out

           cars into the noisy busyness of day.

This longing, again for him, who —

        that June — did not wait for light,

turned his face away from the window &, quietly,

        entered silence.

[I heard]

I heard

how silence swallowed his last breath —

& followed him

inside the silence after that.

[Arroyo Burro Beach]

Arroyo Burro Beach. The tide dies a while

then starts its way up again —

& up again.

Fog rolls in, dense & sudden. Behind me

there's a rock halfway to the end

of the bay, hunched,

split in two, black & blue with mussels —

that's where I turn around & walk

back each day. A restlessness

swells inside the tides there —

& it's there each time, just before I can look

away — then, everything drowns

into itself again & into gray.

I no longer pick up shells — I let them be. Waves

      rake them back & place them

           at my feet again anyway:

small skeletons, dead, but pretty.

Look at me, writing circles around

      what I must face:

      the man I love is dead.

The ashes he asked I lose to this ocean are still

      in our room, in a red box

      he gave me, for some birthday, in New York.

His dust. I'll keep it a while longer. I'll keep it

      as one secretly keeps something

      for one's self

& won't, today at least,

lose more of him to these waves.

[Clouds heave]

Clouds heave over the mountains, rip

      && rain — at last. Years of drought,

            yet spring drenches everything

with jasmine stars & citrus blooms.

The hummingbirds are drunk. All night,

            the mockingbird. Each dawn

the call & call of crows.

      (His widow, for five years tomorrow)

At first, no tears. Everything I was told

            would happen as I mourned,

      didn't. No sobs, no rage,

            no stage one, two, three.

No welcome dreams in which he'd appear.

            His cat mourned better than I, lying

on her side for weeks across his room's threshold,

stretched as much as she could,

back paws against one side

of the doorjamb, front paws to the other.

She waited for him. I paced the house, the streets.

No tears. I cleaned & sewed

& raked & wrote. Sat in the jacaranda's

shade as its shadow soaked the orchard.

Walked the beach. Stooped for stones —

how they'd huddle in my palm: a white one tarred black,

the one like a fist,

& another with a hole bored

straight through its center.

I threw them back. The metaphors too blatant.

Nights, I'd walk from the kitchen to the orchard

    & measure it, one foot in front of the other,

        head bent, toes to heel, heel to toes,

           whispering numbers.

           Thirty-four feet wide.

           Thirty-three feet deep.

& still, no tears.

[There was a room in Antwerp]

There was a room in Antwerp I loved so much

      I never filled it with books, a bed, or a table.

    It was alive with its own clarity — & I feared

anything left there would etch shadows in that radiance.

The room was in the attic of a hundred-year-old house.

    Hunched under a mansard roof, all its windows

faced the sky. No horizon, no walls, no other windows

      stared into mine.

The wide-planked floor had been painted over for more

    than a century. Scratches in the floor revealed other

      colors under its white surface. A deep scuff

showed a reddish gray, other scratches yellow, green, or black.

    The sun splashed into that room at noon:

cascades of light. Dust, sucked upward by the heat,

fluttered under the skylight's chicken-wire glass.

I'd stretch out my palms to the rays then,

    & grab that light, lie on my back & listen —

through the layers of whirling air — to the city's guttural chatter,

the clang of tramways, & melancholic calls of tall ships

        with their crowns of shrieking gulls.

        I owned that light — alive in my hands.

[So, how are you?]

So, how are you? friends ask, all kindness & concern,

        heads cocked, eyes locked in mine.

&, just like that, I'm his again:

        his wife, his widow: the one whose name

was hyphenated to his — & I'm oddly

        happy to speak about

myself, coupled to him again, finally,

        & say I'm okay, better, but won't say

his name out loud yet because I know

        I'd throw a shadow over the conversation —

all kindness & concern — & over him also,

        who no longer has a shadow.

[The empty room I loved]

The empty room I loved led to a larger one, where I lived.

On the floor, by my bed, askew on a stack of books,

    stood my small transistor radio. It caught

        three stations:

        one was a pirate radio, broadcasting

from a ship in the North Sea.

    The other, with Flemish news, only came on

        two hours each night, & the one I listened to

    most was a classical music station.

It played, uninterrupted, for an hour or more,

    then, after a minute or two of absolute silence,

        a woman's weary voice.

She must have been in her late eighties

           & constantly stumbled

    on musicians' names. I can still hear her say

"Rack-mun-num-nee-noff."

Every hour, Our Lady's Cathedral chimed a while —

then the treble bell rang the hour.

I'd stand on a chair, lean through

a dormer window to watch

how Our Lady's steeple pierced the light.

Summer of '63. I was free, I was twenty.

I fell wholly & forever in love every week.

I was hungry for life & satiated by it,

reading deep into the night, & copied

Sartre, de Beauvoir, Apollinaire, Gide, Rilke,

Baudelaire, Senghor, Goethe,

Rimbaud, & Lorca in my notebooks —

barely sleeping before I rushed

down to work, then ran back

    up the five steep flights

        to that white, lit room.

[I was twenty then]

I was twenty then & remember how in stores,

tramways or cafés, I'd catch someone's gaze:

eyes that took me in &

held me there

for an instant. The glint of those stares —

a flash of mica — offered to me & just like that,

my loneliness

shattered.

Everything was light: those eyes, that gaze —

Then, just as sudden, I

disappeared again

inside the dismissal

of a blink.

I'd search again & again for other eyes, other heart-gasping moments to take me in, hold me —

it didn't matter how briefly

as long as

I was held.

(& yet, with him, when — from across a crowd, table, or pillow — his gaze

took me in — it was I who looked away first. Oh.)

[Some nights]

Some nights, settled against him, my face in his neck, I missed him
— feeling that he was elsewhere.

I bought a new bed after he died, his imprint in ours unbearable
— now that he was nowhere.

[How can I say]

How can I say this, if not in the simplest way:

Often, I loved to hear — no, listen to — his sleeve's

shush on our table.

[Some evenings]

Some evenings, he would hide his face in his hands

    for a few seconds —

then let go of his held breath

       & lift his head again, his eyes bereaved

of light.

    What room, face, gaze haunted him?

& where you are, friend, in

    Kansas

    Utah

    Rhode Island or

    Tennessee —

what haunts you? What is it

you choke inside your palms?

Have you told someone? Have you? Will you?

[I had weeded]

I had weeded, hemmed, counted,

raked, cleaned. I had written myself

reminders: I needed

to wash the curtains. I had

a knot of thistles in my throat,

I couldn't swallow. Swallow,

swallow, I'd say aloud.

      I was asleep when he died.

      I did not wake when he died.

I stood in his orchard. Heard

the wind stuff night into the tree.

I thought of his clothes. I had

stuffed them in a plastic bag &

vacuumed the air out of it:

I had sucked his air out of his clothes.

I walked to Las Positas Road,

to Peregrina Street, to Pueblo.

From Pueblo up to Stanley,

back to Las Positas. I remembered

to wash the curtains. I remembered

to feed the cats.

      I was asleep when he died.

      I did not wake when he died.

I broke the brown bowl he loved. I had

filled it with water for the birds.

Four years of drought & the birds

were dying — the hills too. No

clouds. California was burning.

I turned off the radio, hearing this.

I squeezed my thumbs in my fists.

      I was asleep when he died.

I had to go, I had to leave —

I couldn't remember for what.

I couldn't remember for where.

I drove North on the 101, in the dark,

to Refugio Beach.

I listened to Dylan:

She left with the man

with the long black coat.

I made a U-turn —

        I did not wake when he died.

The mountains are

filled with lost sheep.

I counted the cars I passed

(fifty-two, plus seventeen

trucks & a bus) drove past

our house to Stella's Café:

he loved to go there

for Happy Hour, he & I

loved to walk there,

he & I, we'd —

& then — there, welcome

in the café's parking lot —

the tears.

[Horse hooves, Flemish jabber]

Horse hooves, Flemish jabber, & tugboat hoots

ruffle the air. A Sunday in summer. The skylight is open,

so are the windows. The transistor crackles a piano piece.

I sit in the lit room, by the door, my back to the white

brick wall — & layer by layer by layer, peel

away the floor paint in a corner of the threshold.

Paint petals in my palms. A hundred

years of lives, a hundred keys to this door: a thousand

kisses under the chicken-wire skylight, a century

of slammed doors, babies' cries.

Women, men, couples moving in, choosing

a color for the floor. Moving out,

leaving scuffs & scars behind.

The color gray was for a stevedore I knew

who read North Sea clouds better than God, but couldn't

read or write.

The blue for a boy thumbing his marbles

in the grooves between the planks.

Green for the lovers who rushed upstairs, laughing, breathless,

then walked back down so silently.

But the black paint? The black for the sirens of May 1940.

Hitler's *Blitzkrieg* blanket-bombing Antwerp —

his *Luftwaffe* ordered to

avoid Our Lady by all means:

Hitler loved her: he wanted her for his *Reich*.

Then this thin layer — a dusty yellow.

For the Jews.

It can only be for the Jews.

For their yellow armbands under black Stars of David.

For the Jews cattled to the *Breendonck* Transit Camp,

sorted, separated,

beaten, starved, shot

in *Breendonck*: only fourteen miles

away from my white, lit room.

[Dusk at the end]

Dusk at the end of the old stone pier. Pelicans

    dive deep into the waves as we had into each other.

I stand here, remembering that, but can't

    remember his body's weight on mine.

That man I knew by body & skin & belly & heart —

    I have — so soon — forgotten his weight on me.

[Then, you stop]

Then, you stop weeping. Lift your face from your hands.

Not because you're done or because it helped,

but because there's a faint knock at the window.

You look up. It's a branch. It taps & waves & distracts

your sorrow. You wipe your face

hard with both hands.

This is not a sign. You're ruefully aware of that, & don't

believe in signs. They announced a storm,

it nears. That's all.

Yet the sky is so still — so lit. Again, those knocks

at the window. It's not him.

Of course it isn't.

[For weeks now]

For weeks now, no thistles in my throat.

I clean & count & sew & write & rake.

I walk the ocean's hem & hum a little.

I pick up stones, bring them home: one

tarred black, one with a hole in its center.

I sit by the jacaranda, hold stones in my lap.

I'm cold. It's late, the sun fades,

but just before it turns its back to me,

it wraps a ray around my shoulders, finds

my hands & warms them: weighted,

worn, old, open & lit.

III

THE NIGHT GARDEN

Because everything you learned from the stained

        glass windows you knelt under

still remains thorned & stained & torn,

& all the teachings you were expected

        to believe still leave you dis-

believing &

you wish this were not so,

& because one sparrow's chirp can pour

        gratitude into you like drought-

dazzling rains, & you'd much rather

kneel for that — & you do,

there's something appeased in the way you

get up again & brush the dirt

from your knees — that modest

dirt that belongs to no one & is yours so entirely

in this small lot — hedged, hidden,

      with its offerings of fruit

& shade & song. So that later,

when evening brumes embrace all

      you just praised,

you slip back into the night garden

to be blessed that way too.

OCEAN ROOMS

The moon trawled the low tide far back behind the beach,

    beyond black rocks, into a shimmer of gravel

& beach glass: a Klimt rug of green, amber, gold,

    hidden most of the year in the ocean's backrooms.

But it's winter solstice & a large sun is all chilled

    radiance this morning. The tourists are gone,

the locals still asleep or on their way to work, so the ocean

    throws open its rooms for me alone, lays bare

a million splinters & shattered deaths: shells & boats

    & glass & bones, letting the sun stun them

with air & light. All of this such wonder & wreckage,

    unburied alive between sky & sea.

I'm glad for this beach, glad for its tides, for things

that do come back.

Just as I leave — coming close so eagerly —

a back-lit wave swells, rises, curls, &

drowns this instant back into its kelp-choked rooms.

THE PULL

So that, at the end of the morning, when I kneel

at the tide's pull, it suspends its tug to

give me time to drown

my wrists in it.

The wind knots my hair, the sky wild with curlews,

godwits, & gulls. They don't trust me,

they soar & soar away.

I remember unknotting

my daughter's hair once, & hurting her.

How — startled, weeping — she buried her face

in my belly. She was a frail thing, so thin.

Isn't this how I am now, frail, my head

full of knots, wanting to be hidden

inside the ocean?

No, no, not to drown, but to be rocked

inside it for as long as it takes to want to breathe again.

The tide

recedes, I hear it scrape the sands

back into its gray graves. Some days waves are

transparent, clear as a trusting child,

but today they're too busy knotting their long manes of kelp.

It is time to look up again.

Watch a sail catch the light & wind &

see nothing but that: light sailing toward me.

ROBERT'S KEYS

Silver — a gleam on the corner of Constance & State

yesterday — three keys,

        Robert printed on a tiny dog tag.

What woman once chose his name, as she stroked

her pregnant belly — who whispers

        his name to him today?

I walk, at low tide, along this mussel-gleamed, breeze-

stroked beach. His keys in my hand.

        They will never open anything for me.

        ...

Because they belonged to others & because I will never

know their story, I pick up

        buttons, gloves, ticket stubs —

consoled that I own some small thing from other lives & am

linked to them — & belong

to their brief glint here, to their dying.

...

Those keys now against my skin for an instant of impossible

intimacy, no one here to see me:

an old woman who mourns still, paces

a beach, useless keys in fist, as waves open &

lock their large doors &

she hums a small song to herself, almost joyful.

LIVING ROOM, MEMORIAL DAY

These garden flowers sit too pretty in the living room:

  they're the only thing alive in its dust &

stuffiness, so I bring the bouquet outside,

   to the table under the tree & let it

take in the light.

Let those flowers be for that very old man

   I can't forget, who wept —

hunched on a park bench — as he pushed a dead

   sycamore leaf round & round with his cane.

Let them be for the crows, finally

   quiet this morning, & the black

rats as they slink up & down the fig tree.

For the dying daylily — although the day isn't dead yet.

For the candles lit, then left to die

        on ten thousand soldiers' graves.

For the charred smell of meat the neighbors

        flip as their daughter sings

a cannibal king with a big nose ring to her stuffed dolphin.

        How no one will remember this moment,

the street aflap with flags & cookout-frantic,

        while I, mercifully mortal like all of this,

        sit by a table with flowers, & — invisible still —

rot slithers up their young stems.

I FORGET TO LISTEN

To the silence after the rain,

after a slammed door,

or a telephone's last ring.

& to the silence in you, friend.

I make such noise, such noise,

that I forget to hear the silence in you.

BEDROOM

Light puddles over the old floor planks,

                climbs the wall behind

what his place was in our bed, & glows there.

Slow, past noon, jacaranda shadows

                   douse that light & push it

out of the room. Every day.

As if they know he won't come back.

Then reds, golds & grays ooze into

                 the clouds' great rooms

while dusk — all tact & hesitance —

loiters by the door, & — for you, for me,

for my neighbor in his yellow raincoat

                 & plaid pajama pants,

& for who is inside that ambulance yowling

down the 101 — light, dying, curls up

        inside night's wide-open arms.

SUNDOWNER WIND

Three days now & the sundowner stubborn: a hot hiss

in the jacaranda. It's in bloom. There is no blue

    like this one, dusted by drought & dusk

        but flowering all it can —

raising its fists to the other blue — up there — sun-fraught,

    contrailed, hazed & exhausted with light, but there,

        unfailingly there.

    The streets are empty, but for a mockingbird on a roof, he too

        doing all he can, singing to the scorched mountains

pockmarked by the Tea Fire.

The sundowner danced

        with that fire for days,

    its flames still a rage in my old friend's eyes:

    she lost all she had to it.

I think of her often, bent over, sifting

    pottery shards from her house's ashes & finding

        solace there. My god: solace — in so little.

The sun's down. The wind dies in the tree.

    I thumb the two wedding bands on my finger, have them

        do their little dance together: shy rings

    in a stillness that can't silence everything.

ELEGY ON MY DRIVE HOME

for Larry Levis

When it rains on Las Positas Road,

    the trunk of a eucalyptus there turns

      blue — with a few blood-red streaks — but mostly

        blue: a bright

        hard cobalt,

      & it just stands there, bleeding that blue,

among the other eucalyptus in their safe

        camouflage of beige & brown —

& I remember something Larry wrote about Caravaggio,

    how he painted his own face

        in the decapitated head of Goliath,

    & how Larry wanted   *to go up to it & close both eyelids*

      because they were   *still half-open & it seemed a little obscene*

                    to leave them like that.

I planted a willow in a garden in Belgium when Larry died.

It grew by blue-painted shutters. I wanted that tree

     to keep weeping there after I left for America again —

America who had lost Larry too — & I thought about that,

              & about his two trees, lost somewhere

     in Utah: the *acer negundo*, & the other one

whose name he could never remember.

     So that now, when I drive home I think of those trees:

the *acer negundo*, the other one, & my willow.

Brother limitation races beside me like a shadow too, Larry,

     so that now, when it rains, I take

another way home, or look

away from the Las Positas eucalyptus

standing there soaked & bleeding so

blue. It's a little obscene to leave it like that.

POSTCARD WITH AN AERIAL VIEW OF NEW YORK

Friends,

To think that each of those windows

tells a story in this city's Great Book.

A few lines — not pages, not chapters —

written by us all. He & I met some

of you in those rooms, loved many.

Elbows on wine-freckled linens,

we ate & drank at tables humble &

bold. Feasted, we wrote our own fiction

or tentative truths. Some of you opted

out, or away. Others slipped their names

over yours in doorbell name-holders.

You found us in this city, him & me, writing

our banal, beautiful & forgettable story.

Him & me. Him & me.

LET THAT BE PLENTY

are the last words in the book I close

        now, its cover a blue

    aflame in my hands. I hold it

against me, look up for the first time in hours.

The cat's curled at my feet. The fan still

      stirs the curtains. I walk

        out, let the late afternoon

sun wrap its dying around my shoulders.

Night — that light-swiper — is still

      a while away & I'll let that

be enough, & plenty.

WHILE THERE IS STILL TIME

let me waste it, take it outside & do nothing

but sit with it under the old vine's nave

       & its chaotic choir of sparrows.

It's one of those days when nothing gets done,

       my head a constant whinge of worries.

But a breeze drifts in from the East & inside it the distant peal

of church bells then — from the past, a shiver: a line

       from Apollinaire: *À la fin tu es las de ce monde ancien.*

       You're tired, finally, of this ancient world.

I had forgotten it for so long

       & here —

       six thousand miles away from Paris

       six thousand miles from a room in Antwerp

where I memorized "Zone" by heart —

I hear myself say it aloud

to a dusty congregation of sparrows.

...

Some poems will never leave me — they are my other mother

tongue — their scansion the beat in my wrists & throat.

...

But these sparrows: how easily they come & go

from gnarled darkness into bright noon light,

& how, if there is no water, they'll bathe in dirt.

...

I watched a woman once, on a subway platform, grab

her screaming child's wrist, twist it, & shake her,

pointing to a cat-sized rat chewing at something

between the rails: *Stop it or I'll throw you to that rat.*

That woman. She seemed so defeated, so beat.

That child. Her terror as she wrapped herself

around her mother's legs: *I stop, mama, I stop.*

I recognized that terror — my whole body a gasp: it was

a station of my childhood, there, not three feet away,

as the train screeched out of the tunnel. I didn't board it.

Joined the crowd toward the EXIT & its urban dispersal,

all of us strangers, worn, torn, mute, blinded by New York's

noon, its chaos & roar — brief companions in a scattering flock.

...

The sparrows haven't stopped their commute & —

again — it's Apollinaire I remember:

You almost died of sorrow then,

A Lazarus bewildered by light

& as the birds bathe in their fonts

of dust & sun, another line:

Un instant voile tout de son ardente cendre

(An instant veils everything with its ardent ash) —

but I can't remember

        what came before that line,

or after. It doesn't matter:

there's such perfect unimportance here,

        my memory so generous, untangling

lines & languages as I sit by a vine,

wasting time & taking my time to do so.

THIS NIGHT

It wouldn't take much on a night like this, to walk

into it & wear it, be cloaked with it,

disappear into it, the stars barely visible

above the oil rigs off the coast, aglow like phantom ships.

Instead, you pick up the old cat who brushes

against the rosemary. She complains a little — you inhale

that perfume in her fur so wildly.

Such lassitude about her: tired of being

the only living thing in the house with you,

tired of how you need to hold her against you, too tight,

before she wrests herself out of your arms

to disappear into it — this night.

ACKNOWLEDGMENTS

To the editors of Poem-a-Day at the Academy of American Poets, *Askew,
Connotation Press, The Cortland Review, The Enchanting Verses, Gamut,
Miramar, The Louisville Review, Permafrost, Plume Anthology, Plume Online,
Sungold Editions, The Wide Shore*: thank you.

Thank you Martha, thank you Ryan, thank you all at Four Way Books.

Là, au cœur de mon cœur : Mathieu, Maelle, Sara, et Tibo.

My arms around you, Nickole Brown & Jessica Jacobs.

Such gratitude for the indispensable friendship of Miles & Mimi Coon,
Janlori Goldman & Katherine Franke, Tony Hoagland,
Steve Huff & Betsy Gilbert, Meg Kearney & Gabriel Parker, & Charlie &
Helen Simic.

For your stalwart loyalty & friendship, thank you James Anderson,
Bazza Burchell, Stephen Dunn & Barbara Hurd, Iannemanneke,
Eugenia Leigh, James Lenfestey, Martinneke, Lewis Owen,
Kamilah Aisha Moon, Ginger Murchison, Aidan O'Brien, the Roahen
family, Mary "Marieke" Ruefle, Tim Seibles, Carine Topal, Brian Turner,
Chase Twitchell.

To my caring West Coast friends, I'm deeply thankful for your solid,
attentive shouldering during what were difficult years: Gudrun Bortman,
Mary Brown, Chris Buckley, Elena Karina Byrne, Pamela Davis,
Marsha de la O, Carol Decanio, Kim Dower, Nancy Gifford,
Catherine Hodges, Lois Klein, Christine Kravetz, Wendy Larsen,
Jackie LeGuellec, Perie Longo, Enid Osborn, Diana Raab, John Ridland,

David Starkey, Phil Taggart, Emma Trelles, Bruce Willard, Paul Willis, & George Yatchisin & Chryss Yost.

May Wednesdays continue to be such perfectly fitting patterns of solidarity and laughter, dear sewing companions.

And such gratitude for the community of writers at the Solstice Low-Residency MFA in Creative Writing Program of Pine Manor College: my second family.

For my students everywhere, who continue to teach me: thank you.

How I miss you, Brigit Pegeen Kelly, Larry Levis, Thomas Lux.

...

"The Night Garden" is for Nickole Brown & Jessica Jacobs.
"The Pull" is for Owen Lewis.
"Robert's Keys" is for Janlori Goldman.
"Sundowner Wind" is for Gudrun Bortman.
"Let That Be Plenty" is for Nathan McClain.
"While There is Still Time" is for Miles & Mimi Coon.
"This Night" is for Steve Huff & Betsy Gilbert.

...

In the poem "Elegy on my Drive Home," the italicized lines are quoted from "The Perfection of Solitude: A Sequence" by Larry Levis.

In the poem "While There is Still Time," the italicized lines are my translations of lines from Apollinaire's poem "Zone."

Laure-Anne Bosselaar is the author of *The Hour Between Dog and Wolf* and *Small Gods of Grief*, which was awarded the Isabella Gardner Prize for Poetry in 2001. Her third poetry collection, *A New Hunger*, was selected as an ALA Notable Book in 2008.

She is the recipient of a Pushcart Prize and her work has been widely anthologized. Garrison Keillor read four of her poems on NPR's *The Writer's Almanac*. She is the editor of four anthologies: *Night Out: Poems about Hotels, Motels, Restaurants and Bars*; *Outsiders: Poems about Rebels, Exiles and Renegades*; *Urban Nature: Poems about Wildlife in the Cities*; and *Never Before: Poems About First Experiences*.

Bosselaar has taught at Emerson College in Boston, Sarah Lawrence College in New York, and the College for Creative Studies at the University of California, Santa Barbara; she is a member of the founding faculty at the Low-Residency MFA Program at Pine Manor College. She also offers private mentoring and poetry editing services.

Publication of this book was made possible by grants and donations. We are also grateful to those individuals who participated in our 2018 Build a Book Program. They are:

Anonymous (11), Sally Ball, Vincent Bell, Jan Bender-Zanoni, Kristina Bicher, Laurel Blossom, Adam Bohanon, Betsy Bonner, Mary Brancaccio, Lee Briccetti, Jane Martha Brox, Carla & Steven Carlson, Caroline Carlson, Stephanie Chang, Tina Chang, Liza Charlesworth, Andrea Cohen, Machi Davis, Marjorie Deninger, Patrick Donnelly, Charles Douthat, Emily Flitter, Lukas Fauset, Monica Ferrell, Jennifer Franklin, Helen Fremont & Donna Thagard, Robert Fuentes & Martha Webster, Ryan George, Panio Gianopoulos, Chuck Gillett, Lauri Grossman, Julia Guez, Naomi Guttman & Jonathan Mead, Steven Haas, Lori Hauser, Mary & John Heilner, Ricardo Hernandez, Deming Holleran, Nathaniel Hutner, Janet Jackson, Rebecca Kaiser Gibson, David Lee, Jen Levitt, Howard Levy, Owen Lewis, Sara London & Dean Albarelli, David Long, Katie Longofono, Cynthia Lowen, Ralph & Mary Ann Lowen, Jacquelyn Malone, Fred Marchant, Donna Masini, Catherine McArthur, Nathan McClain, Richard McCormick, Victoria McCoy, Britt Melewski, Kamilah Moon, Beth Morris, Rebecca Okrent, Gregory Pardlo, Veronica Patterson, Jill Pearlman, Marcia & Chris Pelletiere, Maya Pindyck, Megan Pinto, Taylor Pitts, Eileen Pollack, Barbara Preminger, Kevin Prufer, Vinode Ramgopal, Martha Rhodes, Peter & Jill Schireson, Jason Schneiderman, Jane Scovel, Andrew Seligsohn & Martina Anderson, Soraya Shalforoosh, James Snyder & Krista Fragos, Ann St. Claire, Alice St. Claire-Long, Dorothy Tapper Goldman, Robin Taylor, Marjorie & Lew Tesser, Boris Thomas, Judith Thurman, Susan Walton, Calvin Wei, Bill Wenthe, Allison Benis White, Elizabeth Whittlesey, Rachel Wolff, Hao Wu, Anton Yakovlev, and Leah Zander.